LIFE IN A DAY OF BLACK L.A.

The way we see it

LIFE IN A DAY OF BLACK

L.A.

The way *we* see it

L.A.'S BLACK PHOTOGRAPHERS PRESENT A NEW PERSPECTIVE ON THEIR CITY

EDITED BY **ROLAND CHARLES** AND **TOYOMI IGUS**

ESSAYS BY **HOWARD BINGHAM** AND **J. EUGENE GRIGSBY III**

TEXT BY **TOYOMI IGUS**

PHOTOGRAPHY BY:

NATHANIEL BELLAMY

ROLAND CHARLES

DON CROPPER

CALVIN HICKS

JEFFREY

MIKE JONES

KAREN KENNEDY

ROD LYONS

WILLIE MIDDLEBROOK

AKILI-CASUNDRIA RAMSESS

PRODUCED BY **UCLA CENTER FOR AFRO-AMERICAN STUDIES** AND

BLACK PHOTOGRAPHERS OF CALIFORNIA

DESIGNED BY **WESTWORK DESIGN**

◄ The view of Los Angeles from the African-American community of Baldwin Hills.

PHOTO BY **ROLAND CHARLES**

Library of Congress Cataloging-in-Publication Data

Life in a day of Black L.A.: The way <u>we</u> see it: L.A.'s black photographers present a new perspective on their city /
edited by Roland Charles and Toyomi Igus; essays by Howard Bingham and J. Eugene Grigsby III;
photography by Nathaniel Bellamy . . . [et al.];
produced by UCLA Center for Afro-American Studies and
Black Photographers of California ; designed by Westwork Design.
p. cm.
(CAAS special publication series, ISSN 0882-5300 ; v. 8)
1. Afro-Americans—California—Los Angeles—Social life and customs—Pictorial works. 2. Los Angeles (Calif.)—Social life and customs—
Pictorial works. I. Charles, Roland. II. Igus, Toyomi. III. Bellamy, Nathaniel. IV. Black Photographers of California. V. University of
California, Los Angeles. Center for Afro-American Studies. VI. Series.

F869.L89N35 1992   92-28435
979.4'9400496073--dc20   CIP

Center for Afro-American Studies
University of California, Los Angeles
Copyright © 1992 by The Regents of the University of California
First printing
All rights reserved

ISBN 0-934934-38-X (hardcover)
ISBN 0-934934-39-8 (paperback)
CAAS Special Publication Series ISSN 0882-5300, vol. 8
Printed in the United States of America

This book has been published in conjunction with the exhibition *Life in a Day of Black L.A.: The Way <u>We</u> See It*, organized by UCLA Center for Afro-American Studies and Black Photographers of California, and serves as the catalogue for the exhibition.
Front cover photo: "Eye on L.A.: Florence and Normandie, May 1, 1992" © 1992 Jeffrey.
Back cover photo: Windsor Hills Elementary School pupils © 1992 Mike Jones.

▼ Street musician performing on Venice Beach.

The conundrum of color is the

inheritance of every American. . . . It is a

fearful inheritance, for which untold

multitudes, long ago, sold their birthright.

Multitudes are doing so until today.

—*James Baldwin*

◄ **Eleven-year-old Aaron Gonzales waits**

for the right wave at Venice Beach.

FOREWORD
by the editors

The old adage "seeing is believing" is simply an early observation about the power of imagery, proven time and again throughout the history of photography. Without photographs, the world may never have believed the horrors of the Holocaust or, recently, the suffering in Somalia and the abuses occurring in Sarajevo. Had the centuries of enslavement been documented through photographs, it would be much harder for America today to forget and dismiss the effects of those atrocities on Black America and its psyche. Perhaps the "conundrum of color," as James Baldwin put it, would cease to be a riddle.

While the lack of documentation and images about the plight of African peoples was, in retrospect, harmful, the fictionalized pictures of Blacks coming from Hollywood were perhaps more damaging. The myths about Black people may not have been born here in Hollywood, but from here they spread all over the land and beyond. With the advent of television, these fictional images were suddenly being served to and ingested by Americans right in their own living rooms. Yet these images were, more often than not, accepted as truth: After all, aren't all the "good" Black people happy-go-lucky day laborers who lead useful lives cleaning up the world for white folks to rule? Enter Bill Cosby and his ground-breaking television show and professional and lay critics alike were quick to debate how "believable" the show actually was.

Not that pictures weren't ever being used to tell the "truth." Film and photography revolutionized the print and television news media. If a picture is worth a thousand words, why not use splashy, sensational photographs to capture the ever-decreasing attention span of the American public? Pictures may not tell the whole story, but they do not lie.

Or do they? Ironically, the jurors in the Rodney King case might say that they do. And as L.A.'s infamous film industry knows all too well, pictures may not lie, but film can create fibs. Impressions can be formed, then changed, then reformed again and again merely by manipulating what it is we see.

The absence of a true reflection of African Americans on film has been exacerbated also by the lack of opportunities for and acknowledgment of Blacks behind the camera. Although Black photographers have been active since the middle 1800s, capturing, among other subjects, Black life in America, only a few have been deemed "masters" of photography and none of the history books even footnote the contributions of notable pioneers, such as Jules Lions of New Orleans or

James Presley Ball of Ohio. Since Black Americans have never been in control of the mass media, we have—like all other minorities—become victims of its manipulation, be it deliberate or unintentional. Without the power to oversee the depictions of ourselves, we remain half-formed half-truths in the minds of most. The Sambo image of the early movies may have evolved (though this is, to some, debatable), but new stereotypes have formed: Black youths are all gangbangers; welfare recipients are Black single mothers too lazy to work; Black men do not support their families; the list, sadly, goes on.

Los Angeles is the home of the entertainment industry, the source of much of what the world sees about America. While it is considered to be the media capital of the world, it is also perceived to be one of its crime capitals, where drugs, violence, and poverty are pervasive. Caught between these two extreme scenarios are the African-American people, particularly the Black residents of L.A., who become defined by the new stereotypes created by and then disseminated from this city.

However, out of the ashes of the 1965 Watts rebellion came a commitment to change and an awareness of self that engendered photography's emergence as an instrument of social consciousness. The camera became the tool for recording the struggle for equality and preserving African-American history and culture.

In this tradition, *Life in a Day of Black L.A.: The Way We See It* is an attempt to redress the negative imagery of Black people that bombards viewers daily. Ten of Los Angeles' African-American photographers focused their cameras on our Black communities and recorded a perspective on our lives that is generally not seen. The resulting work, arranged here as an imaginary day in the city, is the first photographic look at contemporary Black culture in the West. It is also a long overdue acknowledgment of the talents of L.A.'s Black photographers.

It must be understood that no single exhibition or publication could possibly tell the entire complex story of Black life in Los Angeles, and we don't even try. We simply offer this project as a gesture of friendship and as an invitation to the concerned and the curious to come and visit our house. See life the way we see it and see how similar we all really are.

—The editors

◄ Toyomi Igus *(left)* is the managing editor of UCLA Center for Afro-American Studies Publications. Photographer Roland Charles *(right)* is the director of Black Photographers of California.   *Photo by Mike Jones*

PHOTO BY DON CROPPER

...HE IS HERE
TO REALIZE GREAT THINGS
FOR HUMANITY, TO ATTAIN
NOBILITY AND TO SURPA
VULGARITY IN
EXISTE

INTRODUCTION

by Howard Bingham

In my struggle to become a photographer, I was fortunate to have had the opportunity of documenting the lives of the rich and famous, the world shakers and newsmakers. However, I have achieved a greater measure of success because my skills were recognized by two of America's greatest living Black men, Muhammad Ali and Bill Cosby. Since the 1960s I have shared special moments in the lives of these two men. Both succeeded against great odds, broke down racial barriers, and exhibited an unwavering dedication to their craft and to their people. Their experiences, as well as my own, unmasked the struggles of all African Americans in our fight for equality and recognition. With my camera I was allowed to participate and contribute to that struggle.

The battle continues.

In 1965 the people of Watts rebelled against oppression and poverty. News editors the world over wanted me to shoot pictures, but I was traveling with Muhammad Ali and was not in Los Angeles, the town I call my home. However, another opportunity presented itself in 1966. Another disturbance broke out. It was my coverage of this small uprising in Watts that year that led to my being hired by *Life* magazine. Once a part of their staff, I was sent to document the protests and civil uprisings—"riots," if you must—that were occurring all across America over the next few years.

Then and now, being a photographer who is Black has some advantages as well as tremendous responsibilities. People gave me safe passage through the community and a picture of their lives not given to photographers who are white. I could cover an US meeting in the morning, a Black Panther meeting in the afternoon, and an SCLC rally at night. Even though these groups were political rivals, they all trusted me.

There were also disadvantages: In 1968, Bill Cosby hired me to be the photographer on the set of his new television show. I was denied entry into the still photographers union, which was required if I was to work on the set. Cosby insisted that I work on the show and, so that I could, he paid a stand-by union photographer to do nothing for 18 months. Two years later, the Equal Employment Opportunity Commission mandated that Howard Morehead, an African-American cameraman, and I be allowed in the union, two of the first Blacks ever to be afforded membership.

And still the struggle continues.

◄ **Caretaker at St. Elmo Village, a community arts facility and studio complex.**

I have covered some of the most historic moments of the civil rights movement and seen much change in my life. I have traveled with the greatest and broken bread with the poorest and most underprivileged. I have covered freedom marches in the South and the North, rebellions in Watts and Detroit. I rode with the Mississippi Freedom Riders, and witnessed with my camera the funerals of Martin Luther King Jr. and other civil rights leaders. Much has changed for the better with regard to the plight of African Americans, but sadly there is still much to be done. True acceptance and understanding, which nurture equality, are in sight but still out of reach for people of color. There is work still to be done. This is why I was so deeply honored to have been asked by this fine group of photographers to introduce their book, *Life in a Day of Black L.A.: The Way We See It.*

Photography has given me an appreciation of images and their power to effect change. We saw the power of photography at work in 1965 and '66 when we captured the Watts rebellion on film. We saw the power at work in 1988 when politicians plastered the image of Willie Horton on television screens across America. We saw the power of photography at work this very year when once again Los Angeles erupted with the frustrations of a disenfranchised people. We see the power of photography at work every single day when images of African Americans in handcuffs, on welfare, and in prison are used to illustrate our social ills, but seldom to capture our dreams or articulate our promise.

That is why when I look at this fine collection of photographs I see those all-too-rare images that attest to the beauty and strength of African Americans. In these pictures I can see the hope and love and creativity that lie within my people. These pictures tell a different story from those presented to America by the mass media. They tell a larger, more complex story of a people who, after more than 300 years, are still strangers to most Americans. Conceived in love and understanding, these pictures have the power to heal and nurture a country that is still in search of its identity. The language they speak goes beyond color and culture; they embrace all humanity in sepia tones.

Photographers who are Black bring to the art of photography a unique perspective, because the product of our work represents the sum total of not only our life experiences, but of the entire history of our people. Through our camera lens comes our own unique reflection of our own unique reality. We see things that others cannot simply because we love who we are. The true story of Black America cannot be told unless our voices are included, unless our vision is shared. This is what makes *Life in a Day of Black L.A.* that much more extraordinary.

For the children of Los Angeles—brown, red, yellow, black, and white—these pictures are even more essential. The city that they will inherit is a model for the emerging world. We must arm them with values that celebrate diversity and that find challenge and wonder—not fear and distrust—in the unknown. They must know that most young Black men are not gangbangers or drug abusers, that the Black family is strong and supportive, that African Americans—as doctors, lawyers, equestrians, postal workers, nurses, singers, artists, teachers, farmers, laborers—have heavily invested in this country, emotionally and economically, and have much to contribute to its future.

On the surface, this seems like a simple desire, easily achieved. But we must not underestimate the negative power of the media or the lasting influences that have shaped the lives of the parents of these children and their parents before them. The images presented in *Life in a Day of Black L.A.* celebrate a world we all inhabit, and all of the photographers involved can take pride in the fact that they have joined the ranks of James van der Zee, Gordon Parks, and Roy de Carava when they recorded both the beauty and the pain of Black America. Let these ten West Coast photographers now join those East Coast greats and become our voices from the other side of America.

The battle may continue, but I am heartened when I can count on these photographers as my brothers and sisters in arms, our cameras as our weapons.

—Howard Bingham

▶ World-famous photographer Howard Bingham is perhaps best known for his celebrity photographs of Muhammad Ali and Bill Cosby. He is currently working on a book about Muhammad Ali, featuring photos culled from his lifetime's worth of memorable pictures of the Champ, to be published by Simon & Schuster.

Photo by Roland Charles

Black Los Angeles refers less to a particular

community than to the collective consciousness of the African-American people

of Southern California. Black Angelenos reside everywhere:

from Culver City to Compton, Westwood to Watts, Pasadena to Palms. Some

of us live in extreme affluence, others in suffocating poverty. But all of us rise

each and every day with a goal, a plan to make our mark upon the world—

in one way or another.

As the sun rises over East L.A. and heads towards the ocean, the day begins

for most of us the way it does for folks anywhere else in the United States:

with the newspaper, a hot cup of coffee, or an early morning jog. . .

PHOTO BY **JEFFREY**

BACKGROUND PHOTO—**DON CROPPER**

PHOTO BY **KAREN KENNEDY**

▶ **The family that jogs together stays together: The Holiday family exercising in downtown Los Angeles.**

▲ Dancer Chiko Floyd warms up before his morning run.

aking advantage of the beautiful

climes of Southern California, we head outdoors

before the smog descends. . .

BACKGROUND PHOTO—ROLAND CHARLES

PHOTO BY  JEFFREY

r before the grown-ups awaken.

Determination: Six-year-old Kitara

Ramsess awakens and goes out to shoot

some hoops before the day begins.

▼ Yolanda Parker, businesswoman, combs daughter Kimberly's hair before
carpooling the neighborhood kids to school.

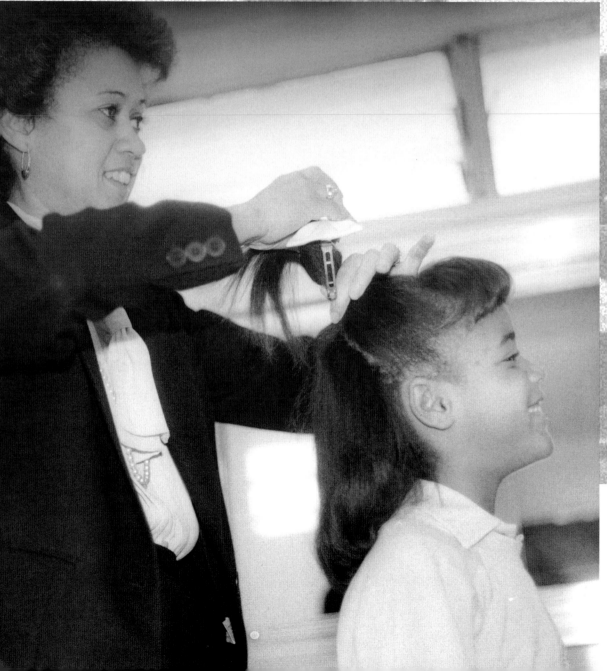

Then, fortified, we prepare

to face the world.

▶ The Baldwin Hills two-career couple: His-and-her Benzes.

PHOTO BY MIKE JONES

▲ Extended-family support: Lorine Hall cares for her granddaughter Vanessa.

Traditionally,

African-American women

have always worked outside

the home—in the fields,

in the factories,

as servants who provided

leisure and quality time

for others—

so juggling job and family

responsibilities and finding

(and affording) loving day care

for our children are not

new dilemmas for the Black

family. Whenever possible,

we rely heavily on extended-

family support.

▲ Rochelle Nicholas-Booth, artist and
educational coordinator at the Watts Tower
Arts Center, with her son Lorenzo.

PHOTO BY **WILLIE MIDDLEBROOK**

BACKGROUND PHOTO—**KAREN KENNEDY**

▲ George Wheaton has been driving the new Rapid Transit District (RTD) Blue Line train for

about two years. He has been with the company for over 23 years.

▼ **Sumire Gant of the community affairs office of the RTD, at the 103rd Street Blue Line train station in Watts.**

R

egardless of where we

work, each of us must

contend with L.A.'s

infamous commute—

by car, bus, or train. . .

► Letter carrier,
Eighth Street and
Broadway, down-
town Los Angeles.

PHOTO BY NATHANIEL BELLAMY

BACKGROUND PHOTO—AKILI-CASUNDRIA RAMSESS

hether we are employed by the post office, attend school at Dorsey High, run our

own small business, or are partners in a law firm, the goal of the day's work for

most African Americans is simply to improve the quality of our lives.

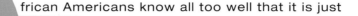

African Americans know all too well that it is just not enough to perform up to the "norm." Blacks must perform better and should still not expect to be rewarded as greatly as our white peers. Since the time of our enslavement, we Black parents have taught our children that education is the key and knowledge the weapon that will overcome the ever-present obstacles of prejudice. For centuries we were denied access to even the most rudimentary of educations. Today many of us are still denied access to equal education. Yet we persevere and try to give our children the best we have to offer while we teach them those lessons and skills that cannot be learned from any textbook: how to survive in a society that is, at best, merely tolerant of and, at worst, hostile to our very existence.

PHOTO BY MIKE JONES

BACKGROUND PHOTO—MIKE JONES

PHOTOS BY **NATHANIEL BELLAMY**

ℬut at least for a while our children

can be children—blessedly naive and innocent.

Toddlers at Para Los Niños, a preschool in downtown Los Angeles.

BACKGROUND PHOTO—KAREN KENNEDY

▲ **Early morning girl-talk at the University of Islam at Mohammed Mosque #27 on Western Avenue.**

Despite our common heritage and history, the African-American community is wonderfully diverse, and the education of our children comes in many forms. . .

▼ Students at the University of Islam file off to class.

O verseeing these daily lessons are the teachers, who have long held highly respected positions in the African-American community. Black teachers have always been our beacons of light, guiding Black children to a better life.

◀ Brother Reginald X, teacher at the Marcus Garvey school.

▲ Alexina McIver reprimands one of her sixth graders at the 78th Street School.

PHOTO BY AKILI-CASUNDRIA RAMSESS

► A student in
Ms. Beverly's
fourth-grade
class at
the Marcus
Garvey School.

hile the pollsters, scholars, and the media focus their attention on the

school drop-out rate of inner-city children, we must not forget to praise the efforts of

those who have prevailed and to applaud the fact that for every child who

drops out of school, six remain.

PHOTO OF DR. AYIM PALMER, DIRECTOR OF THE MARCUS GARVEY SCHOOL—AKILI-CASUNDRIA RAMSESS

PHOTO BY **KAREN KENNEDY**

◄ Robert Davidson at his East L.A. factory, Surface Protection Industries, which grosses over $40 million in sales annually.

hen statistics show that the

African-American middle class has grown by almost 400% in the past three decades, it is

not news to Black Angelenos. After all, Los Angeles is the home of some of the most

highly visible and affluent Blacks in the country. However, the questions remain:

Why are Blacks on average still earning less money than their white counterparts? Why is

it still so difficult for Black business people to get loans and establish credit? Why is the

corporate "glass ceiling" an all-too-painful reality for our Black professionals and

managers? Ask any of the working people on the following pages if they have ever

experienced discrimination on the job or while trying to run their businesses,

and their answers would be a unanimous "yes."

Yet you will find all of these folks at the height of their typical work day

shouldering such burdens and continuing on as they strive to achieve.

◀ Attorney Artis C. Grant Jr. prepares to close a deal at his downtown corporate law firm, Grant and Duncan.

PHOTO OF WANDA WALLACE, ART DEALER—JEFFREY

▶ Award-winning journalist Pat Harvey, coanchor of KCAL-TV's nightly news show, is L.A.'s only Black prime-time daily news anchor.

▼ Deejay Cliff Winston on the air at FM92.3, the Beat.

hile L.A.'s film and television industries are only partially open to Black writers, producers, and directors, Los Angeles' music industry is less shy about employing, supporting, and exploiting the talents of African Americans. After all, they understand that the urban youth are their primary audience, and that music is the messenger for the young.

▶ Foster Corder,

music video

producer for

Capitol Records.

PHOTOS BY **AKILI-CASUNDRIA RAMSESS**

BACKGROUND PHOTO—CALVIN HICKS

▼ Shopowner on Central Avenue.

*S*outh of the glitz and glamour

of Hollywood, workers of a different ilk struggle to make

their living doing what they know how to do best.

▼ Junkyard proprietors on Central Avenue.

▲ An Altadena beauty parlor.

▶ Neighborhood barber in Pasadena.

Getting ready for the weekend.

◄ Owner of a newsstand at First and San Pedro Streets, downtown.

◄ Dollmaker Maria Brown Scoggins also teaches Afro-American studies at El Camino College.

▲ Lonza Lester gives Jelani Ferguson trumpet lessons amidst the jazz album collection of Jelani's father.

▲ Novelist Joe Nazel at work at home.

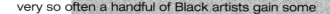

Every so often a handful of Black artists gain some

national—and usually short-lived—attention. They are primarily film, television, and music personalities. But

Los Angeles, the entertainment capital of the world, is also the home of a great number

of fine sculptors, painters, photographers, and performers whose work is often overshadowed by the

attention given to our resident popular-culture superstars.

In the decade following the 1965 Watts rebellion, several Black-owned art galleries and

two African-American museums were organized. Black art in Los Angeles had found a forum. Despite the

fact that support from the greater Los Angeles community is woefully lacking today, cultural institutions

like the Watts Towers Arts Center, the California Afro-American Museum, the Ebony Showcase Theater,

and Crossroads Theater continue to provide some sustenance and much emotional support to our local

artists, most of whom are also sadly neglected by the East Coast-based art and theater establishments.

PHOTO BY DON CROPPER

PHOTO OF WATTS TOWERS—ROLAND CHARLES

CAUTION

◄ John Outterbridge,
artist and director
of the Watts Towers
Arts Center, in front
of his sculpture
entitled "Window
with Ball," which is
installed in a
Pasadena business
complex.

PHOTO BY **ROLAND CHARLES**

D

espite the lack of

financial, spiritual, and emotional

rewards, Black artists like these continue

to communicate the frustrations and

fears, dreams and desires

of the African-American people

through their uncommon creations.

PHOTO OF DALE EDWARDS' METAL SCULPTURE, "THE JUNKIE"
—ROLAND CHARLES

▲ Sculptor Dale Edwards removes his sheet-metal sculpture,

"The Third Son," from a gallery on Rodeo Drive, Beverly Hills.

◄ Artist Pat Ward Williams in her Los Angeles studio.

▶ Artist Toni Love in her Compton home/studio putting the finishing touches on her painting "Sistuhs" for her one-woman exhibition at the Watts Towers Arts Center.

▲ Siris Ani Hetepsek-Unaan, artist and clothing designer, in her Compton home/studio standing in front of some of her art work.

▲ Cedric Adams, Compton-based artist, in front of his graphite drawing entitled "Adam and Eve."

▶ Oliver Muldrew, pioneering community photographer, who founded the 43-year-old Photo Hobby Club.

BACKGROUND PHOTO—ROLAND CHARLES

58

PHOTOS BY ROLAND CHARLES

Black photographers have been active since the middle of the 1800s. The camera became a tool with which we could record our struggles and preserve our history and culture.

▶ Photographers Bob Douglas (front) and Coleman Grimmette (rear) at work copying photographs for the Los Angeles Public Library archives.

▼ Actor Darrow Igus in character as Zeke, an elderly Black Hollywood janitor/day actor, from his one-man play, *Zeke: A History of Blacks in the Movies.*

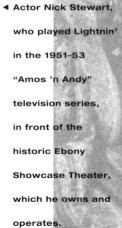

A

frican-American actors

have been seen on the silver

screen ever since *Birth of a*

Nation, Hollywood's first major

motion picture, was released.

Their presence has always

influenced—for better and for

worse—popular perceptions

about Black Americans, and

many, many fine actors call

Los Angeles home.

◄ Actor Nick Stewart, who played Lightnin' in the 1951–53 "Amos 'n Andy" television series, in front of the historic Ebony Showcase Theater, which he owns and operates.

PHOTO OF THE LATE JOEL FLUELLEN, ACTOR—ROLAND CHARLES

E ven though Black Angelenos have

a wide variety of skills and interests, we do not always find gainful employment.

We do not need another survey to tell us that many Black workers never

received the education and training needed to compete in this society; that hiring

practices around the country and across the board are biased; that Black

employees are often the last hired and the first fired. Motivated and influenced by

a culture that encourages consumption and self-indulgence, Americans—

Black and white—when faced with the prospect and/or realities of

poverty sometimes turn to crime, drugs, or both. The majority of us,

however, somehow manage to remain law-abiding citizens, who struggle

to do the right thing even when hardship befalls us. . .

◄ Homeless artist in front of the
Museum of Contemporary Art,
downtown L.A.

PHOTO BY NATHANIEL BELLAMY

And for every tale of crime
and violence, there are ten of faith and perseverance.

HOMELESS PEOPLE SEEKING WORK—ROD LYONS

◄ Homeless man
registering for
jobs at the Job
and Housing Fair
in Inglewood.

▼ At the time this picture was taken, this family was living out of their car.

The parents were signing up for work at the Job and Housing Fair.

or every sad story about

the effects of poverty and

homelessness, there are

dozens about dignity in the

face of adversity.

▲ This woman calls the car her home on Central Avenue.

PHOTO OF PERSON SLEEPING ON BUS STOP
BENCH—CALVIN HICKS

And for every victim of drug abuse

there are hundreds of accounts of drug

recovery and survival. Perhaps when our

society is able to tell the difference between

poverty and the poor, drugs and drug addicts,

crime and criminals, we will be able to finally

deal with the root causes of our social problems

instead of focusing primarily on their effects.

▲ Funeral of a young man at

Inglewood Cemetery.

▶ Marionette Anderson, a drug addict for over 20 years, is now recovering and is the director of a drug rehabilitation center for women in Compton.

The common goal of humanity is to solve the riddle of the

meaning of life. Most of us look for clues to the puzzle through our churches and spiritual

guides. This has always been particularly true for African Americans, and the Black people of

Los Angeles are no different. The physical distance that exists between all of L.A.'s communities

exacerbates our economic and social distinctions, creating for many Angelenos a

feeling of emotional and social isolation. Black Angelenos are able to cope with this

situation in many instances through our churches, which can serve as meeting

places, community centers, town halls, and, at times, social clubs.

We are a deeply religious people, who have found more than spiritual

nourishment in our churches. There we can speak freely and candidly

with those who share our experiences and understand.

GREATER PAGE TEMPLE, CHURCH OF GOD IN
CHRIST, LOS ANGELES—ROLAND CHARLES

BACKGROUND PHOTO—JEFFREY

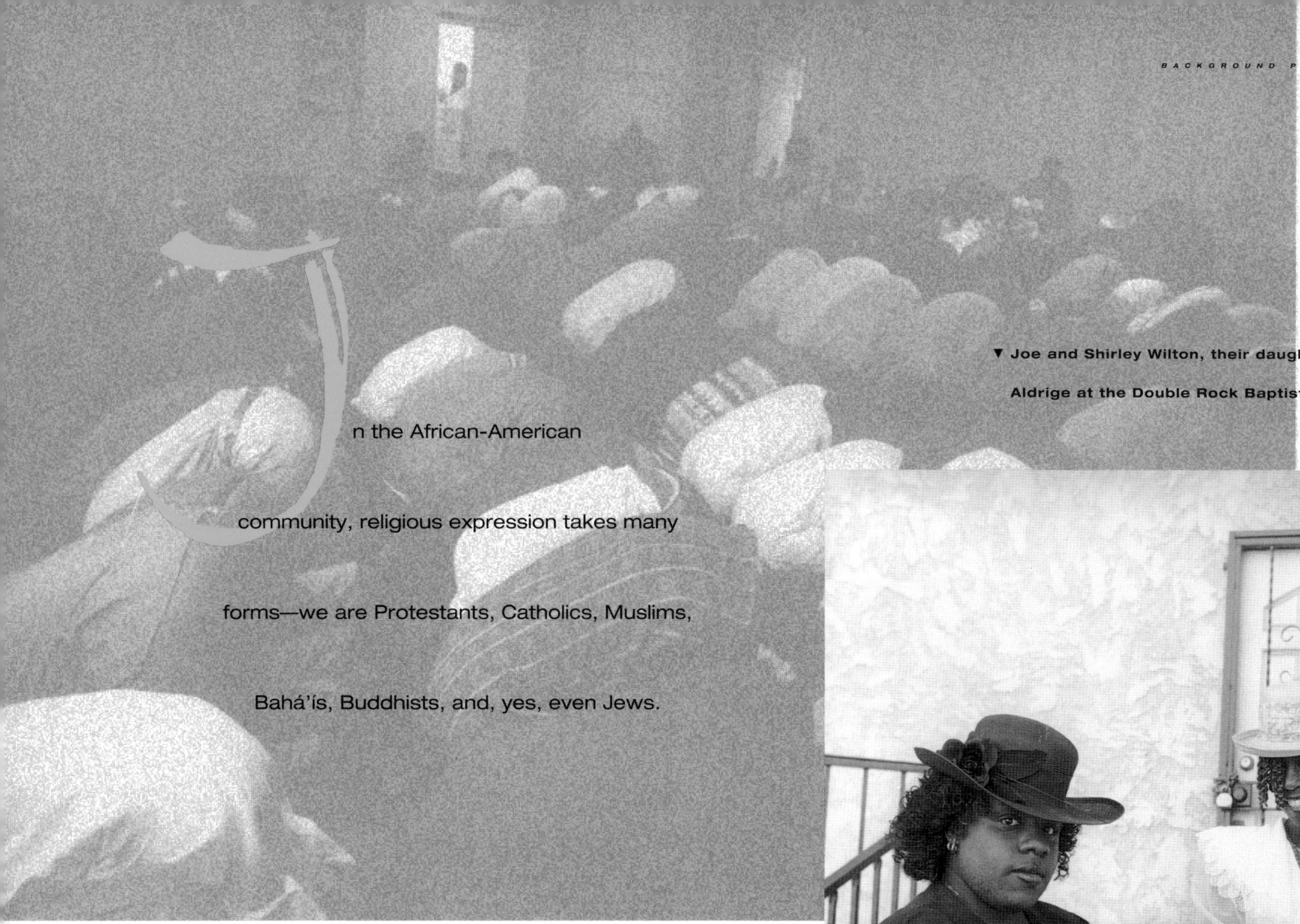

In the African-American community, religious expression takes many forms—we are Protestants, Catholics, Muslims, Bahá'ís, Buddhists, and, yes, even Jews.

PHOTOS BY JEFFREY

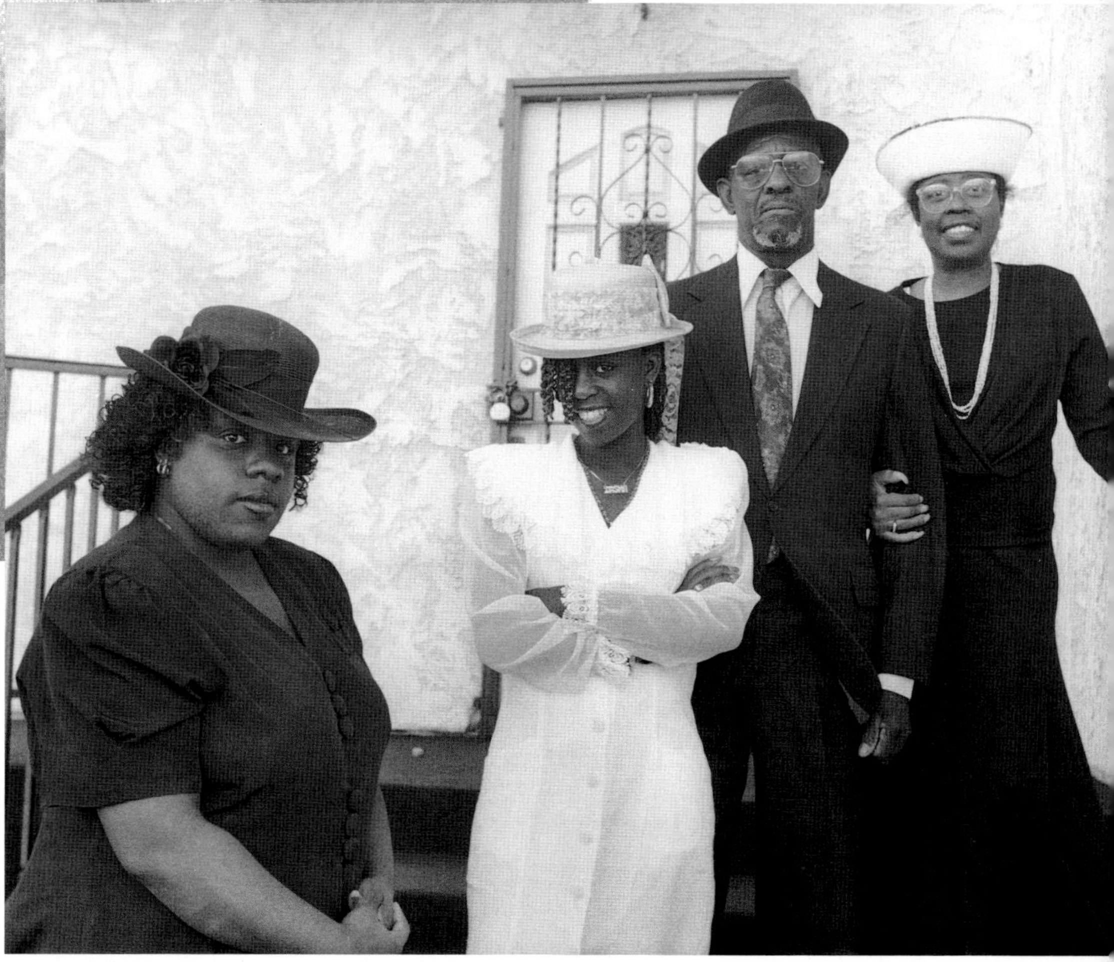

◀ **Men at the Central Avenue Mosque in South Central Los Angeles.**

▼ **Joe and Shirley Wilton, their daughter Tasha, and friend Darnetha Aldrige at the Double Rock Baptist Church in Compton.**

▲ Young man reading a Bible on a Crenshaw Boulevard street corner.

utside of organized religion,

some of us take to the street

to search for answers—or to

provide them.

PHOTO BY NATHANIEL BELLAMY

BACKGROUND PHOTO—ROLAND CHARLES

▼ A storefront minister, who counsels and nurtures the local homeless on Central Avenue.

▼ Bishop Carl Bean, director of the Minority AIDS Project, the first community-based AIDS organization established and managed by people of color.

r sister, I am a person living with AIDS.

...ana, soy una persona viviendo con SIDA.

PHOTOS BY **NATHANIEL BELLAMY**

*BACKGROUND PHOTO—**NATHANIEL BELLAMY***

After a hard day's work, we rest or we play.

To African Americans from other large cities, the lifestyle of Black Angelenos is enviable. Whether they are

modest track houses or sprawling ranch-style homes, single-family dwellings—sporting the ubiquitous

lawn—are a large proportion of the residences of Black families in Los Angeles. Public housing, or

"projects" as they are called in the Northeast, are few. So when we come home to rest, our homes are,

for the most part, welcoming ones—the ever-present urban problem of crime notwithstanding.

The way we play is also different from that of our counterparts in other areas of the country. The most

attractive aspects of Southern California are its beautiful weather year-round and its incredible landscape:

to the west, miles of white sand beaches lay at the feet of rambling hillsides while, to the east, the deserts

form the floor of majestic mountain ranges. Like every other Angeleno, Blacks are quick to take advantage

of—and take for granted—the wide variety of recreational opportunities available to us.

PHOTO BY MIKE JONES

PHOTO OF CARL'S BAR B Q—DON CROPPER

PHOTO BY **DON CROPPPER**

▼ Welcome!

▲ Walking the dog during a Sunday stroll.

PHOTO BY DON CROPPER

PHOTOS BY **AKILI-CASUNDRIA RAMSESS**

▲ The Tiny Mites team of the Culver City Lancers league:

eight-year-old dynamos.

*S*outhern Californian children practically

live outdoors, whether they are participating in organized sports. . .

BACKGROUND PHOTO—AKILI-CASUNDRIA RAMSESS

◄ The Tiny Mites
cheerleaders.

PHOTO BY  ROLAND CHARLES

◄ Eighteen-year-old
Quawan Villary attends
Sherman Oaks High.
He and his friends,
Demetrius (left) and
Jason (center), are
concerned about the
plight of Black youth.

r just hanging out with friends. The particular style

that the rest of the nation considers Californian stems, perhaps, from our young people.

Their fashion sense is as keen and unique as their political outlook—which, at times, overlap.

BACKGROUND PHOTO—KAREN KENNEDY

▲ Youngsters protest the Latasha Harlins verdict at a rally at Compton City Hall.

▲ Aaron Gonzales and his friend Andrew Ruiz boogey-board onto Venice Beach.

In cultivating friendships

in Los Angeles, race is less an issue than the world

may think. Los Angeles began as a settlement of

Blacks, Mexicans, and Native Americans, so the city

can be rightfully proud of its ethnic diversity. To most

of our youth, a friend is simply a friend. . .

▲ After dinner, these friends practice their synchronized ollies as the sun sets on

Saturn Street, mid-Wilshire district.

PHOTOS BY **KAREN KENNEDY**

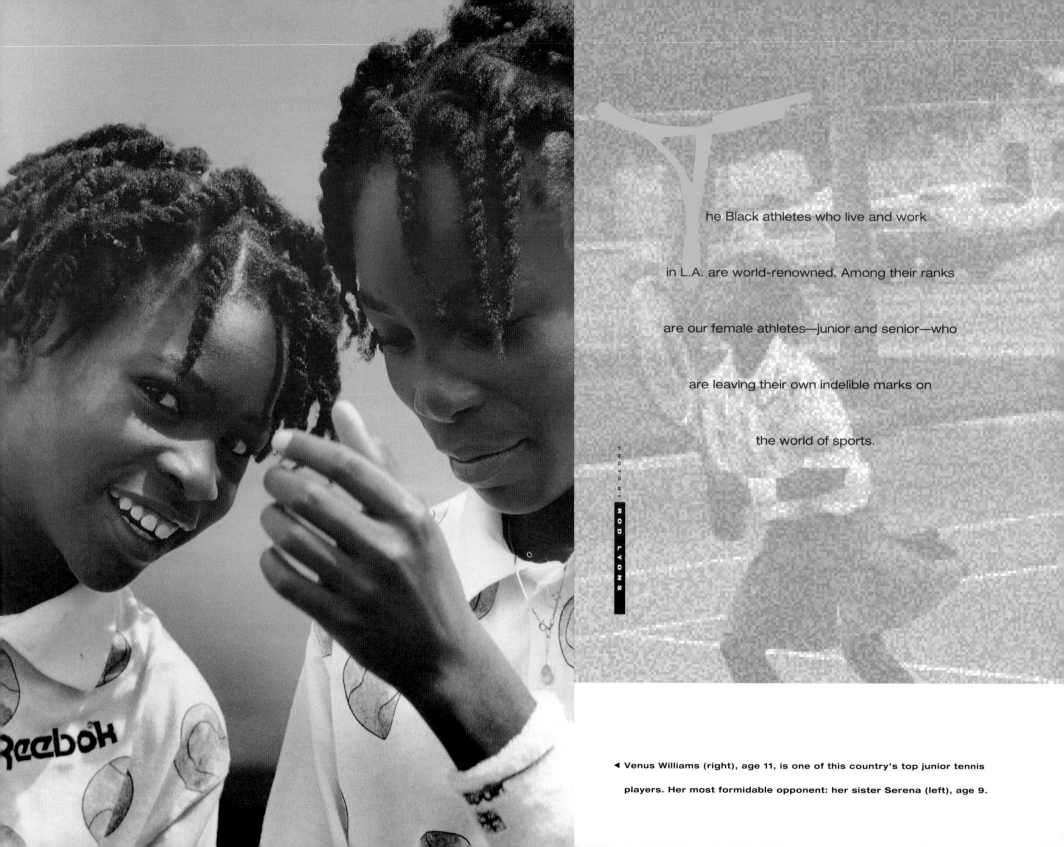

PHOTO BY ROD LYONS

The Black athletes who live and work

in L.A. are world-renowned. Among their ranks

are our female athletes—junior and senior—who

are leaving their own indelible marks on

the world of sports.

◀ Venus Williams (right), age 11, is one of this country's top junior tennis

players. Her most formidable opponent: her sister Serena (left), age 9.

BACKGROUND PHOTO—ROD LYONS

PHOTO BY **ROLAND CHARLES**

▶ Olympian Evelyn Ashford (left) anchors the 100-meter relay team at the annual Evelyn Ashford Invitational Mt. SAC Relays, Mount San Antonio College.

PHOTO BY **KAREN KENNEDY**

E ven the adults cannot resist the lure of L.A.'s beautiful weather. . .

and water.

PHOTO BY **MIKE JONES**

◄ **Kenneth Strauther and Miles**

Frank leave the heat of the

city and go for a spin

on Puddingstone Lake in

San Dimas.

▲ **Former Councilman Dave Cunningham and**

consultant Larry Irvin head out for their

weekly golf game.

▲ Street musician Harry Perry.

▲ A family of Black acrobats show

their stuff at Venice Beach.

▶ One of the many

skateboarders who

frequent the Venice

boardwalk.

◀ Venice artist Robert

Rucker and street ven-

dor Chinike with her

child N'gozikali.

PHOTO BY NATHANIEL BELLAMY

Transplanted Easterners to Southern California bemoan the lack

of seasons with which they can mark the passage of time. The holidays just don't feel the

same, they say. Perhaps that is why Angelenos love a good rousing parade. And after the

Rose Bowl Parade is over and the DooDah Parade is done, Black Angelenos eagerly await

Martin Luther King Jr. Day with all of its attendant splendor.

In similar fashion, we turn out at a variety of other events over the course of a year—

such as the Third World Festival and the successful African Marketplace—to support our

local Black businesses and artists in an atmosphere of pomp and celebration.

◄ Young performers in the King Day parade on Martin Luther King Jr.

Boulevard in the Crenshaw district.

Preparation for MLK Day starts months before and continues up to the last minute.

Some attractions have a decidedly Western slant.

◄ The last of L.A.'s Black cowboy community: African Americans have bred and kept horses at El Segundo and Avalon Boulevards for generations, but new commercial development in the area is forcing the horsemen to either give up their horses or travel great distances to ride them.

PHOTO BY  NATHANIEL BELLAMY

*S*ome participants use the day to announce their accomplishments and their goals.

BACKGROUND PHOTO—ROLAND CHARLES

▲ Actor Jim Brown's organiza-

tion, Amer-I-Can, helps Black

kids stay out of gangs.

*I*t is an

occasion to celebrate

our heritage and our

community. . .

PHOTO BY AKILI-CASUNDRIA RAMSESS

▶ Women waiting for a performance to begin at the Third World Festival.

PHOTOS BY **ROLAND CHARLES**

◀ Actress Cree Summer from NBC's "A Different World" shops the African Marketplace.

J

n all of its representations.

▶ Senior Lead Officer Godfrey Bascom from the Southwest Area Division L.A.P.D.

▼ Los Angeles Mayor Tom Bradley (third from left) with sculptor Charles Dickson (second from left) at the unveiling of the artist's MLK memorial piece in Watts.

LK Day is a time to

remember and to rejoice.

We've come a long

way—yet we've a long

way to go.

▲ Sculptor Charles Dickson with his crew during the

installation of his MLK memorial piece.

PHOTO BY **ROD LYONS**

J t's true. Los Angeles is not a night city,

despite its spectacular nighttime vistas. After a grueling day at work, a long, tough

drive home on the freeways, and possibly dinner with the family, for most Angelenos

there is little time left in the day to get involved in an evening activity.

In the Black community, things are not much different. Although, given the choice of

attending a good event or spending an evening at home watching television, most of

us will go out—if only to see who else is out.

For the teens, a date may entail a movie at the mall, a musical concert, or creative

car cruising on Crenshaw. Older folks might dine out, go to a movie or—occasionally—

the theater, or hit a favorite nightclub to enjoy some live jazz.

BACKGROUND PHOTO—DON CROPPER

▲ Actor Billy Dee Williams with his son at the opening of

August Wilson's "Two Trains Running."

◄ Veteran actor Paul Benjamin

makes an appearance.

► Winnie Mandela and Congresswoman Maxine Waters at a tribute to Ms. Mandela sponsored by the Black Women's Forum at Marla Gibbs' Crossroads Theater.

PHOTOS BY AKILI-CASUNDRIA RAMSESS

◄ African dancers perform at the tribute to Winnie Mandela.

▲ The weekly encounter with the cops.

▲ Wheelies.

▲ Drag races.

◄ Car culture: Sunday afternoons and evenings will find a lot of young car and

motorcycle buffs cruising the Crenshaw Strip.

▲ Watergun fun.

BACKGROUND PHOTO—DON CROPPER

▼ The Dale Fielder quartet, with Nedra Wheeler on bass, performs at the Ellington Room in West Hollywood.

PHOTO BY CALVIN HICKS

▶ Jerry's Flying Fox, a popular Baldwin Hills/Crenshaw nightspot and one of the oldest surviving

Black-owned and -operated supperclubs in Los Angeles.

In the preceding pages we have presented images of Los Angeles the way we see it. Instead of dwelling on the negative, the sensational, or the ubiquitous sports scenarios, ten of Los Angeles' African-American photographers have captured the tremendous range and diversity in lifestyles experienced by African Americans in this city.

Their portrayal of family, for example, shows that Black families exist in a variety of ways: the traditional nuclear unit, the single-parent household, and the extended family household. As different as these families may appear to be, a common thread binds them all: an overwhelming desire to have a good quality of life, a sense of personal security, the ability to secure a job, earn a decent wage, and to have upward mobility. The elderly, while not so concerned with questions of employment any longer, are desirous of some assurance that their ability to receive needed goods and services will not be eroded over time. African-American families also seek reasonable assurances that our selected place of residence will be in a neighborhood where drug dealing does not take place, where the city picks up trash regularly, where needed services are both available and affordable, and where neighborhood schools enable children to be competitive in an increasingly technological society. We also would like to expect that the police will respond to our calls in a reasonable amount of time, believe that the focus of their efforts will be directed at real offenders, and trust that they will not randomly brutalize unsuspecting residents.

The photographers have also captured images of Los Angeles' diverse African-American work force. As can be seen in the pictures, there is a thriving and successful African-American middle class, comprised of workers, professionals, and entrepreneurs. These pictures remind us that, traditionally, African Americans have always held responsible jobs in our community. Images of working novelists, music teachers, artists, actors, and folk artists reflect the great creative and artistic talent that can be found within Los Angeles' African-American neighborhoods.

To be sure, some African Americans, along with a number of other ethnic Angelenos, face difficult times trying to cope with a complex urban environment where lack of appropriate educational skills can inhibit one's ability to obtain a job that pays a decent

◄ Eye on L.A.: Normandie Avenue and Florence Boulevard, May 1, 1992.

wage. Inadequate work skills, coupled with the recent downturn in the economy, reduced to homelessness many African Americans who previously were gainfully employed and capable of providing food and shelter for their families. Changes in governmental policy initiated in the Reagan era and continued under the Bush administration decreased the numbers of those eligible for welfare and further increased the number of homeless African Americans. The pictures our photographers have taken of the city's indigent remind us how African Americans caught up in the poverty cycle are trying to cope.

Another coping mechanism for Black Americans can be found in religion. Religion remains a powerful force enabling us to celebrate joyous occasions and to contend with adversity. In our religious expression we also find diversity: Photographs of Catholic priest Father Burns, the images of Muslims worshipping at the Central Avenue Mosque, and the Baptist family attending a Compton church reflect the various ways African Americans affirm their religious beliefs.

Our photo essay would not have been complete if we had not captured the very essence of Southern California: fun in the sun and rocking at night. From the photos of organized team activities, such as football, track, and cheerleading, to individualized pursuits—surfing, boating, golfing, horseback riding, tennis, and skateboarding—we quickly realize that African-American participation in recreational activities is as varied as the activities themselves.

The epilogue to this book was added to include photographs of the civil disturbances that Los Angeles recently experienced, which began on April 29, 1992. These events occurred as the editors were in the midst of the final edit for this volume. Without any prompting, our photographers once again returned to the streets, this time not to capture a typical day in the life of African Americans, but rather to document—from their unique perspective—the tumultuous events that many believe will inextricably alter life for African Americans and all Angelenos for years to come.

A variety of different essays, news articles, and commentaries have been produced in an attempt to explain what happened this time. While there are differences of opinion as to whether or not a "riot" or a "rebellion" took place, a simple set of facts is known. The African-American community was stunned by the "not guilty" verdicts in the Rodney King case—this coming just months after a probation sentence was given to the Korean grocer who killed 15-year-old Latasha Harlins. Both verdicts served to solidify the belief held by many African Americans that the justice system does not work for them. In addition, our community felt anger because law enforcement officials simply stood by and did not stop the violence. The months of televised replaying of the video that captured the beating of Rodney King by the police officers plus the senseless attack on Reginald Denny served to fuel the rage felt by many in our community. Continuous twenty-four hour live television coverage of the aftermath heightened the media's indications that African Americans were doing most of the looting. In actuality, participants in the disturbance were not just Blacks. Latinos, whites, and others took part in the looting and burning. Statistics, however, indicate that, while more Latinos were arrested than African Americans, more African Americans were killed.

As scholars and policy analysts sort through mounds of data in the coming months, they will undoubtedly recall that many of the same conditions that existed in April of 1992 existed prior to the Watts rebellion of 1965. They are also likely to draw many of the same conclusions that were reached over two decades ago, namely that African Americans, as a group, have higher unemployment rates, less wealth, lower educational achievement levels, and are more residentially segregated than are whites. A major difference this time, however, is that other ethnic groups in our city now share the same plight. The arrest data should serve as a forewarning that a growing group of disenfranchised people of any race, surrounded by wealth and opulence they cannot touch, will only tolerate so much. If people cannot find justice in the courts, access to employment, and/or earn a decent wage, then all of society will be victimized.

The epilogue provides vivid images that relay the messages we need to hear. "Wake Up People" is the plea of some of our residents. But the majority of these photographs remind us that humanism and compassion are not lost among African Americans, particularly during times of personal adversity. As some former gang members seem to say: "We want to be a part of the solution, not the problem. Is anyone listening?"

—J. Eugene Grigsby III

▶ J. Eugene Grigsby III is the director of UCLA's Center for Afro-American Studies, project coordinator of the Los Angeles Mega-Cities Project, and associate professor of urban planning at UCLA.   *Photo by Mike Jones*

PHOTO BY CALVIN HICKS

Like L.A.'s infamous earthquakes, the "not

guilty" verdict in the Rodney King case

sparked a series of damaging aftershocks.

While the emotional eruption

that occurred jolted the entire nation, it

was viewed by L.A.'s Black community as

a disturbing but not unexpected response.

◄ A local resident's plea to her people at a rally at

the Santa Barbara Plaza.

WE DEMAND JUSTICE

► Messengers of the Black Freedom Fighters Coalition in public protest to the Latasha Harlins verdict at a Kwanzaa Day Parade.

Many Black Angelenos—as well as other resident minorities—are frustrated in their attempts to reap the benefits of true equality, and frustration turns to anger and anger to violence when no other outlet is available.

PHOTO BY **ROD LYONS**

◄ **Distributing care packages at the Allen House of the First African Methodist Episcopal Church (First A.M.E.).**

PHOTOS BY **ROLAND CHARLES**

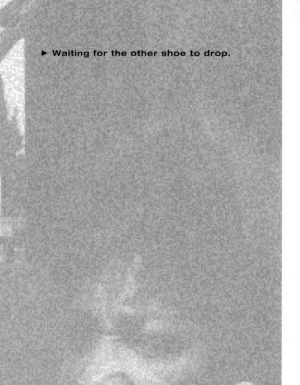

► **Waiting for the other shoe to drop.**

▲ A multiethnic group
of teenagers revels
in the chaos.

J ust as disturbing, however, was how the media incessantly

reported the fires and lootings as Black-on-Black or Black-on-Korean crimes.

PHOTO OF THE NATIONAL GUARD—MIKE JONES

▼ Irony: A Black L.A.P.D. officer and a Black National Guardsman protect an Asian businessman's establishment.

PHOTOS BY ROLAND CHARLES

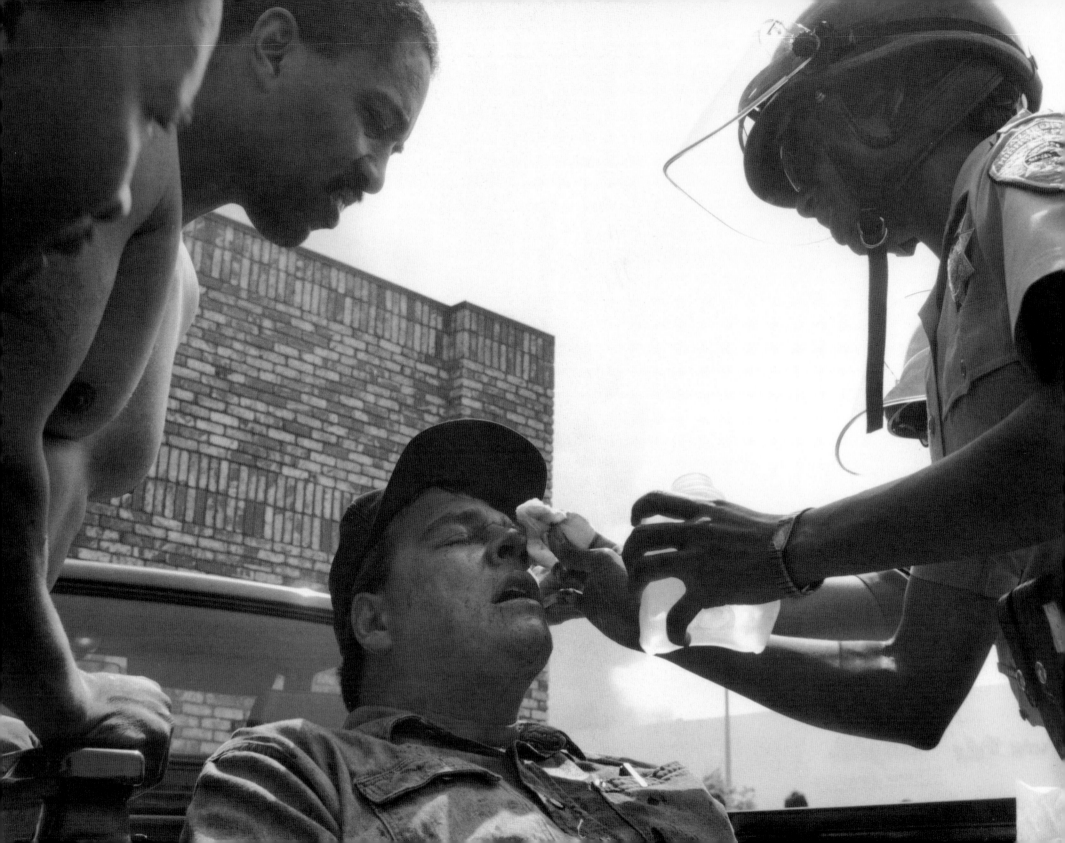

PHOTOS BY **ROLAND CHARLES**

◀ **A Highway Patrol officer tends the wounds suffered by a man who was punched in the face. The two onlookers try to console him.**

▲ **With over 1,100 fires blazing in the city over the course of three days, L.A.'s firefighters had perhaps a harder job than the police.**

▶ View of the injured city from Baldwin Hills.

Signs of the times.

n stark contrast to the widespread

reports of interracial hostility, people of all ages,

races, and communities converged upon churches

like the First African Methodist Episcopal and other

community groups with generous offers of

assistance and expressions of support.

▼ Explain it to the children: A storyteller attends to the children of the volunteers at First A.M.E.

▲ From all across Los Angeles, concerned citizens arrive with food, water, and a desire to

help and to heal.

PHOTOS BY JEFFREY

▼ Chris Tate, the director of First A.M.E.'s young adult choir (right), addresses the fears and concerns of some of the younger congregation.

▼ Rage in paradise.

CRIPS BLOODS
MEXICANS
TOGETHER
LAPD 187

I t cannot be denied

that racial tension exists in

this city, but L.A.'s cultural

diversity leads more often to

vitality and creativity

than to conflict.

▲ "Revolution is the hope of the desperate."

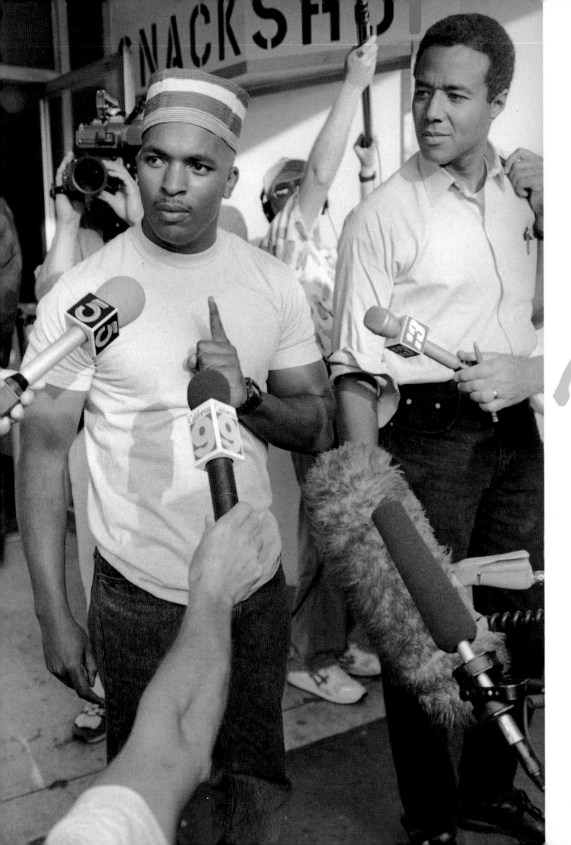

After the uprisings, some gang members, seeking a way

to stop the self-inflicted violence and devastation,

recognized an opportunity to link hands and join forces

towards a brighter future. Pessimists view the

Crips–Bloods truce as an alliance against the police.

Optimists see a ray of light at the end of a dark tunnel.

▼ Trading gang signs for peace signs: The Bloods and the Crips call a truce.

▼ When the smoke cleared, many businesses like the Aquarian Bookstore, this country's oldest continually operating African-American bookstore, were gone. Here, Dr. and Mrs. Alfred Ligon, the owners, survey the damage.

éjà vu: With a little boost from

all of the renewed interest in the problems

facing the inner city, existing community action

groups continue to carry on trying to address

those issues still unresolved from over 25

years ago. Newcomers like the folks at Rebuild

L.A., meanwhile, hope not to repeat the

mistakes of their 1960s' predecessors.

▲ Attorney Rena Wheaton, one of the project managers of Rebuild L.A.,

discusses strategy on how to do just that with project manager

Arnoldo Beltran.

PHOTO BY **ROLAND CHARLES**

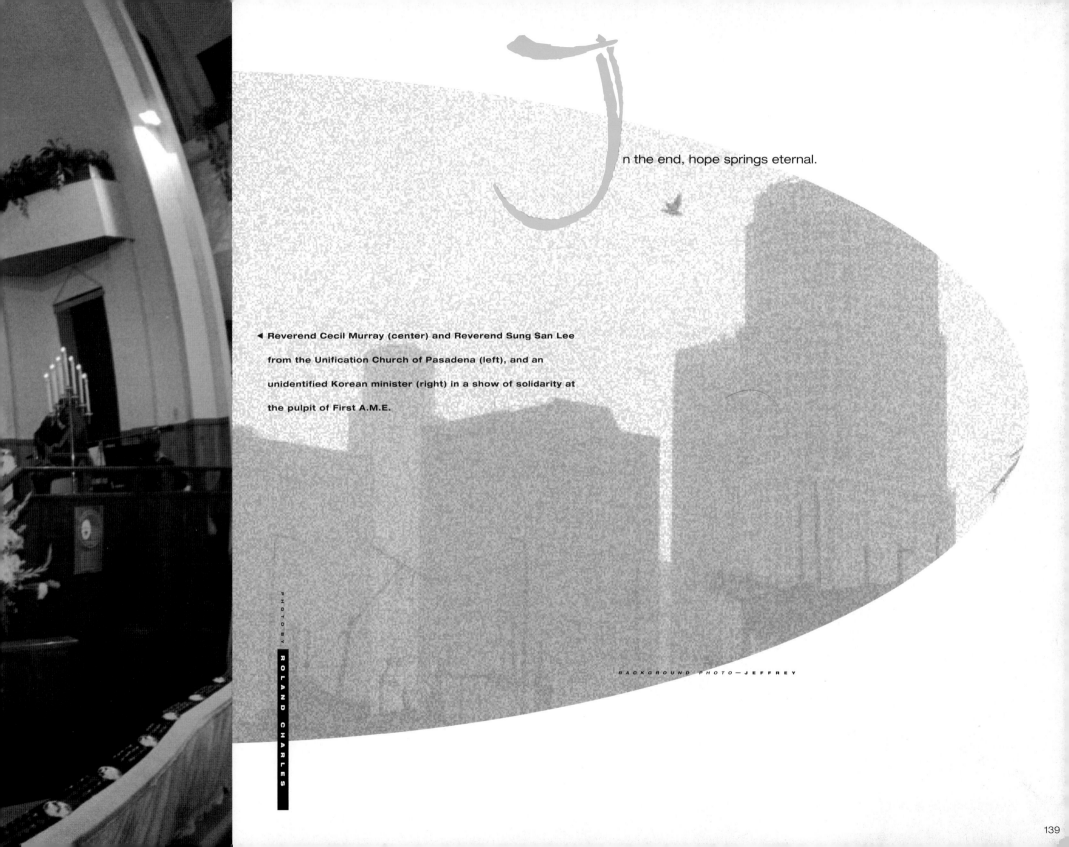

Jn the end, hope springs eternal.

◄ **Reverend Cecil Murray (center) and Reverend Sung San Lee**

from the Unification Church of Pasadena (left), and an

unidentified Korean minister (right) in a show of solidarity at

the pulpit of First A.M.E.

◄ Little dreamers.

ACKNOWLEDGMENTS

The editors of *Life in a Day of Black L.A.: The Way We See It* are indebted to many wonderful people whose unfailing support has nurtured this project from conception to birth.

To all of the people of Los Angeles who allowed us entry into their homes, their hearts, their lives.

To Mayor Tom Bradley, Adolfo V. Nodal, and the L.A. Arts Recovery Fund, a collaborative effort of the J. Paul Getty Trust Fund, National Endowment for the Arts, California Arts Council, AT&T, California Community Foundation, L.A. Art Association, and the Times Mirror Company.

To the UCLA Center for Afro-American Studies, in particular: Director J. Eugene Grigsby III, Project Fundraiser Sandra Sealy, Fund Administrator Jan Chapple, Assistant Editor Ross D. Steiner, Special Projects Coordinator Donna Armstrong, Secretary to the Director Tricia Cochée, Computer Consultant Jonathan Abrams, Editorial Assistants Nicole Hendrix and Stephen David Simon, Intern Christiane Moses, and Librarian Gladys Lindsay. Your tireless efforts will always be fondly remembered.

Extra special thanks to Assistant to the Director N. Chérie Francis, whose unwavering support and generous assistance made the rough times smoother.

To the fabulous design team at Westwork Design, Culver City, Yolanda Davis and Rick Piscitelli, who more often than not were rewarded with pizza rather than pesos.

To the many other kind folks at UCLA who helped our vision become a reality: William Harris at the UCLA Development Office; the UCLA Purchasing Department team of Jack McCoy and Sylvia Wong; Carli Rogers at Contracts and Grants; Harlan Lebo of University Relations.

To Curatorial Assistance's Graham Howe for lending his expertise to the development of the exhibition.

To our loving spouses and families, who have supported us unconditionally throughout it all.

And—most of all—to the following group of fine photographers, who donated their time and their considerable talent to the making of this book:

After extensive training in photography and design at the University of Milwaukee, Nathaniel Bellamy established himself as a professional photographer while a staff member of the University Photographic Service Department. Since his move to Los Angeles, he has divided his time between commercial still photography for the motion picture and advertising industries and his fine art work. Bellamy's photographs have been presented at many shows and exhibits, in such venues as The Milwaukee Art Center, Smithsonian Museum, Los Angeles Museum of Afro-American History and Culture, William Grant Still Community Arts Center, the Los Angeles Theatre Center, and the Black Gallery. In addition, his work has appeared in many major newspapers and magazines.

Bellamy's participation in the *Black L.A.* project was motivated by his belief that one of the root causes of the problems of African Americans is the lack of a positive identity. "Just as change is ubiquitous in society," Bellamy explains, "African peoples in America, I believe, must also change and delete counterproductive concepts—such as the use of the pejorative, 'Nigger.' As long as we as a people continue to define ourselves as *niggers,* we will be considered and viewed as walking contradictions or socio-metaphysical monstrosities. In other words, when we stop using it, they'll stop using it!"

SELF-PORTRAIT—**NATHANIEL BELLAMY**

Life in a Day of Black L.A. is primarily the vision of Roland Charles, a photojournalist and the director of the Black Gallery, a Los Angeles exhibition space, through which Charles actively promotes fine art photography of African Americans and other people of color. He has distinguished himself through his own work as well, which has appeared in national publications, books, and on album covers, and through his continuing support of the arts. Charles is the founder and director of Black Photographers of California, a founding board member of the Jazz Photographers Association, and he sits on the board of the Museum of African American Art and the Los Angeles Center for Photographic Studies. For Eastman Kodak, Charles was the associate producer and host of the television documentary "The Legacy Continued: Black Photographers."

Charles states that he "was motivated to do this project because of a strong desire to set the record straight, to visualize the humanity in Black culture, and to share the perspective of L.A.'s Black photographers with the world."

SELF-PORTRAIT—**ROLAND CHARLES**

DON CROPPER

With more than thirty years of experience in photography and film-making, Don Cropper brings an unusually broad background with him to the *Black L.A.* project. During his career he has been a travel photographer, a cameraman for many major motion pictures and movies of the week (including *Baby Boom*, *Jazz Singer*, and "The George McKenna Story"), and has taught film and still photography in Gothenburg, Sweden. Cropper is also a longtime activist for the cause of equal opportunities for Black photographers and filmmakers: In addition to cofounding the New United Television Movie Equity Guild, Cropper also founded the first Black professional photographers association on the West Coast.

Today two of Cropper's main concerns are the respect and reward that are still to be accorded to photographers by the public. "I am proud to be part of the cadre of African-American photographers who are working as a creative force to assist in change," he says. "My hope for the *Black L.A.* project is that it will increase awareness. Professional photographers are not a dime a dozen. It takes years to perfect our craft and the various industries—and individuals—that use the services of photographers still do not recognize or reward our efforts. If *Black L.A.* can raise the consciousness of people as to the power and value of good photography, then my contribution will have been well worth the effort."

SELF-PORTRAIT—DON CROPPER

SELF-PORTRAIT—CALVIN HICKS

CALVIN HICKS

Calvin Hicks has been fascinated with the camera ever since he first played with one as a child. A fine arts photographer, Hicks has lived and worked in the Los Angeles area for over twenty years. His work has been seen in many shows and exhibits sponsored by the California Afro-American Museum, the Bunker Hill Arts League, and the Frank Lloyd Wright-Ennis Brown House, among others, and has been featured in *Photographers Forum Magazine*'s Best of Photography Annuals in 1983 and 1986 and *Santa Barbara Arts Magazine*. Hicks cofounded the Black Gallery in 1984 with Roland Charles and has since served as curator of many shows featuring the work of established and emerging photographers.

"To my knowledge *Life in a Day of Black L.A.* is the very first publication to deal specifically with the work of West Coast Black photographers. It is an honor to be included in this effort to document life in our community," Hicks says. "This is an attempt to depict all at once the sublime, ridiculous, sacred, and profane aspects of our lives. All of these things make up any community, and when viewed as a collective whole an excellent picture of our cultural tapestry emerges."

JEFFREY

It was during his Air Force assignment in Germany that Jeffrey first attended photo exhibits and became fascinated with photography as an art form. His friendships with a number of European photographers provided him with additional exposure, which was followed by formal training at the renowned Brooks Institute of Photography in Santa Barbara. Jeffrey's work has been featured in the Simon Rodia Gallery, the Cunningham Memorial Gallery, the William Grant Still Community Arts Center, and is part of the permanent collection of the Schomberg Center for Research in Black Culture in New York. He is a director of the Black American Cinema Society and a board member of the Western States Black Research Center.

Of the *Black L.A.* project, Jeffrey says: "I truly enjoyed the opportunity to increase the understanding of my people. Anyone who knows American history knows that at one time Black Americans were not even considered human. I want people not to see us as bad or good, but simply as human."

PORTRAIT—JAMES BROWN

MIKE JONES

One of the younger participating photographers, Mike Jones was a former business student who could not deny his love of photography. He graduated from California State University, Los Angeles, with a degree in art and apprenticed for several years with some of the area's top photographers. A few years ago, Jones struck out on his own and opened up his own photo studio. Since then he has produced album covers for Motown, Warner Brothers, MCA, Atlantic, and Virgin Records, and has become a highly regarded commercial and editorial photographer.

"I can't pretend that I grew up with only one pair of shoes," Jones says of his place as a Black man in America. "I didn't. I grew up the son of a deputy sheriff in View Park, California. I want to show America that Black people are not all destitute and that you do not have to be a dope dealer to own a Ferrari. My father taught me to be self-sufficient and he provided me with the opportunity and the ability to see the world. My contribution to *Black L.A.* is just my way of saying thanks."

SELF-PORTRAIT—MIKE JONES

ROD LYONS

As a photographer and educator, Rod Lyons has been telling stories through his images for more than twenty years. After a six-year tour as a photographer with the U.S. Air Force, Lyons received his degree in journalism at California State University, Long Beach, and went on to establish himself as a photojournalist working for many major publications and as a college-level photography instructor. His work has been published widely both locally and nationally.

Life in a Day of Black L.A. marks a turning point for Lyons in his career. "They say that timing is everything, and the timing of the *Black L.A.* project could not have been better for me. Professionally, a photographic project of this importance and scope is perfectly in keeping with my desire to have my personal photojournalistic voice heard. Also, as a native of Los Angeles, I am very interested in having the whole story of Black Los Angeles told, not just what is shown in the mass media. Through my photographs I want to help people understand that although we are all different, we are all the same. It is my hope that *Black L.A.* will serve as a catalyst for more exploration into the myths and realities of what it means to be an African American—not just in Los Angeles, but throughout the entire world."

*SELF-PORTRAIT—**ROD LYONS***

KAREN KENNEDY

A native of Los Angeles, Karen Kennedy credits her background in textile design for helping to create her artistic vision photographically. Through the use of light, shadow, and subject placement, Kennedy strives to create texture in her pictures. With the techniques she developed through her independent study of art and photography as well as her work in design, Kennedy also relies on her keen observational skills (developed while studying for her master's degree in psychology) to capture unique moments of human behavior. She has taught art at Compton College and has tutored privately. Her photographs have been exhibited throughout the Los Angeles area and can be found in the private collections of William H. Cosby Jr. and Walter R. Hazzard Jr.

"To me L.A. is a huge overgrown town plagued with urban ills but blessed with all of the values of 11 million families," this Angeleno says of her city. "At the base of it all are our children. My photos show hope—the hope that drives young people as they continue to pursue their daily goals, the hope that allows them to accomplish wonders in spite of having to play against a stacked deck, and the hope that springs from the help and support of their families."

*SELF-PORTRAIT—**KAREN KENNEDY***

WILLIE MIDDLEBROOK

Willie Robert Middlebrook is presently the assistant director of the Los Angeles Photography Centers. During his career he has received many commendations from the Los Angeles City Council for his contributions to photography, has been named a Hometown Hero by the City of Compton, and was declared an Outstanding Black Artist in California by Brockman Gallery Productions. Middlebrook has participated in over seventy-five solo and group exhibitions, received a Photographers Fellowship from the National Endowment for the Arts for his documentary "Watts Revisited: Beyond the First Look," and recently participated in the artist-in-residency program at Light Works, Syracuse, New York.

About his work he says: "Art is about communication. I am obsessed with the need to tell, to show what I see, what I feel. I am intrigued and motivated by the human condition and photography is the tool that I use to communicate my feelings. It helps me to seize for permanent record every facet of life that comes before my eyes—from the beginning minutes to those last fleeting seconds. After spending almost all of my preadult and the majority of my adult life seeing negative, nonquality images or no images at all of my people, I decided that there was a need to direct my focus exclusively on producing great images of African Americans; not necessarily in a positive light, but always in a true light. My focus is never limited. I seek to communicate to all willing to listen. Thank you for listening."

*PORTRAIT—*ROLAND CHARLES

AKILI-CASUNDRIA RAMSESS

Akili-Casundria Ramsess' interest in photography began as a teenager when she shot the photos for her North Carolina high school yearbook and moved on to newspaper work there. After moving to Los Angeles, Ramsess received her AA degree in commercial photography at Los Angeles Trade Technical College before receiving her bachelor's degree in journalism from California State University, Long Beach. A talented photographer, Ramsess went on to become a regular contributor to the *Los Angeles Times*, the *Daily News*, the *L.A. Weekly*, a staff photographer of the Los Angeles *Herald Examiner* before its demise in 1989, and the Wave newspapers. She is now a photo editor at the Associated Press wire service. Ramsess' work is also included in the book *Black Women Photographers* (Dodd, Mead & Co., 1986), edited by Jeanne Moutoussamy-Ashe.

"My photographs are a reflection of how I see our people," explains Ramsess. "From the children to the elders—they are all parts of who I am. So the camera becomes my mirror, to reflect that for the world to see. Everything that we have experienced as a people—joy, pain, dignity, the trials we go through—is shown in the faces that I photograph and in the various circumstances in which I find my subjects. When I take pictures, I am always looking for the common thread of humanity that binds us all."

*PORTRAIT—*MIKE JONES

◄ The Black Gallery,

birthplace of *Life in
a Day of Black L.A.*